P9-DXL-044

LAUGH
-OUT-
LOUD
JOKES

TO TELL YOUR FRIENDS

BY MICHAEL DAHL

CAPSTONE PRESS
a capstone imprint

Blazers Books are published by Capstone Press,
1710 Roe Crest Drive, North Mankato, Minnesota 56003
www.mycapstone.com

Library of Congress Cataloging-in-Publication Data
Library of Congress Cataloging-in-Publication data is available on the Library of
Congress website.
ISBN 978-1-5435-0342-5 (library binding)
ISBN 978-1-5435-0350-0 (eBook PDF)

Editorial Credits:
Mandy Robbins, editor; Eric Gohl, media researcher; Tori Abraham,
production specialist

Photo Credits:
NASA: 29; Shutterstock: 5 Second Studio, 9 (cat), Africa Studio, 11, BaLL LunLa, 23,
barteverett, 19 (sign), Elnur, 20, Humannet, 8, Irina Rogova, 7 (toy), Kues, 21 (gorilla &
skyline), Luis Louro, 13, 15, marekuliasz, 24, Milles Studio, 22, Misunseo, 17 (bandages),
MO_SES Premium, 21 (plane), Oksana Kuzmina, 28, Nadezda Murmakova, 10 (otter),
Netfalls Remy Musser, 19 (house), Ricardo Reitmeyer, 30, Pavel Bobrovskiy, 17 (red
bandages), Sergey Nivens, 27, sianc, 17 (ghost), Sirikunkrittaphuk, 31, Tarzhanova, 9
(mittens), Vadim Sadovski, 10 (space), Victor Naumik, 25, Yellowj, 7 (lobster)

Printed and bound in the United States of America.
010877S18

TABLE OF CONTENTS

THE BEST WAY TO TELL A JOKE

What did the lion say after
he ate the comedian?
"I feel funny."

Your friends will all feel funny after
you've told them these goofy gags.
Improve your joke-telling skills by
dishing out the wisecracks. You just
might turn into a world-class comic!

TIPS TO BE A STAND-UP COMIC

1. **Speak up!** No one will laugh if they can't hear you.

2. **Practice.** Rehearse the jokes a few times before sharing them with friends.

3. **Get your timing right.** Your audience will laugh even louder if you pause right before the punch line.

4. **Don't laugh** at your own jokes. Keep a straight face.

5. **Use gestures** and body language. Some jokes are funnier with a well-chosen movement.

6. **Watch other comics.** You can learn a lot from the experts.

JEST FOR FUN

1. Why don't elephants go to the beach?

**Their trunks are
always falling down.**

2. How did the bumblebee get to school?

It took the buzz!

3. Why didn't the little lobster share his toys with the other lobsters?

Because he was shellfish

1. Why did the basketball coach kick
Cinderella off the team?

**She was always running
away from the ball!**

2. What happened at the silkworm race?

It ended in a tie!

A TIE?
NOOOO!

3. Why do ducks fly south for the winter?

It's too far to walk.

4. What happened to the cat that
ate a ball of yarn?

She gave birth to a set of mittens!

1. Where do otters come from?

Otter space

2. Why did the cookie go to the doctor?
It felt crummy.

3. What do you call a train that
eats too much?
A chew-chew

NAME GAME

1. What do you call a girl who likes to play tennis?

Annette

2. What do you call a guy who floats on the water?

Bob

3. What do you call a guy who

hangs on the wall?

Art

MONSTER JOKES

1. Why doesn't Dracula have many friends?

He has bat breath.

2. What did the Loch Ness Monster say to his old friends?

"Long time, no sea!"

3. Why is it safe to tell a mummy your secrets? **It keeps everything under wraps!**

1. What's a ghost's favorite color?
Boo!

2. What did the zombie eat
at the restaurant?
The waiters

3. What kind of fur do you get
from a werewolf?
As fur away as possible

4. What kind of mistakes do
ghosts make?
Boo-boos

1. What do you get when you cross a vampire with a snowman?

Frostbite

2. What do you say to a two-headed monster?

"Hello, hello!"

3. Where does the ghost family live?

On a dead end

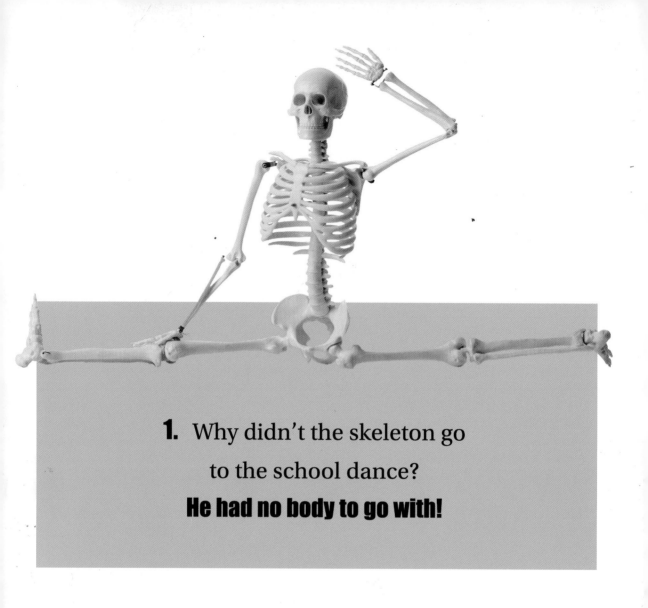

1. Why didn't the skeleton go
to the school dance?
He had no body to go with!

2. How can you tell when
Dracula has a cold?
You can hear his coffin!

3. Why did King Kong climb the skyscraper? **He was trying to catch a plane.**

KNOCK IT OFF!

1. Knock, knock.

Who's there?

Santa

Santa who?

Santa letter telling you

I was coming today!

2. Knock, knock.

Who's there?

Radio

Radio who?

Radio not, here I come!

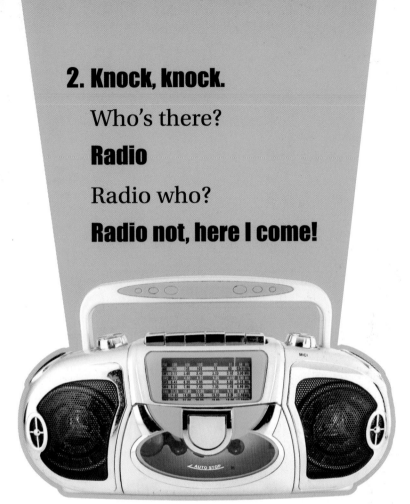

3. Knock, knock.

Who's there?

Isabel

Isabel who?

Isabel not working?

That's why I knocked.

1. Knock, knock.

Who's there?

Canoe

Canoe who?

Canoe come out and play?

2. Knock, knock.

Who's there?

Boo

Boo who?

Oh, stop crying!

3. Knock, knock.

Who's there?

Alex

Alex who?

Alex plain later, let me in!

4. Knock, knock.

Who's there?

Doris

Doris who?

Doris locked, and I can't find my key!

5. Knock, knock.

Who's there?

Noah

Noah who?

Noah a lot more knock-knock jokes!

OUT OF THIS WORLD!

1. How do aliens keep their

pants up?

With an asteroid belt

2. Where did the space visitor

leave her ship?

At a parking meteor

3. How do you get an
astronaut's baby to sleep?
Rocket

1. How can you be sure to have a party that space aliens will enjoy?
Planet

2. What picks up space garbage where no one has gone before?
Star Truck

3. When do astronauts eat?

Launch time

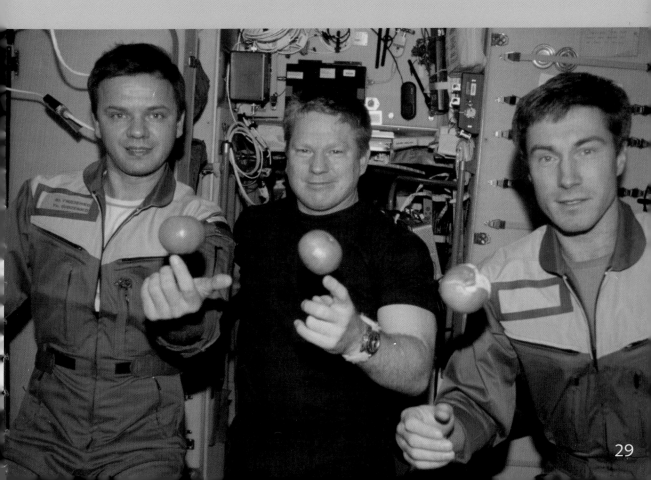

1. Why couldn't the astronauts
land on the moon?
It was full!